Walking in Cemeteries

Amanda Joy Morse

ISBN: 979-8-218-11736-8

To Michael

and to Mom and Dad

for loving me

Contents

Author's Note

After I graduated from college, I started a blog. The plan was to self-publish a novel and to use the blog as a starting point to advertise my new project. But after about five months, I realized that the story I was trying to write wasn't something I was passionate about and so that project died, along with a few others. But the blog kept me writing, and although I wrote less fiction than I intended in the last ten years, what I did write was a lot of poetry.

My poetry is from the heart. I write to work out my thoughts on the page, to try to find understanding in what is happening around me. I've struggled with my mental health for many years and on top of that, I get an extra dose of the blues called Seasonal Affective Disorder around the fall and winter months.

This is where the cemetery comes in. Several years ago, I started a new job and nearby my work is a large cemetery with tall, beautiful trees. On my lunch break and in a bit of a writing slump, I would walk in the cemetery for exercise and amongst the trees, I found my way back to writing and found peace. Many of the poems in this collection are from those walks under the trees, although some are from before as well.

While this collection is from different stages of my life, the poems themselves are also different styles; most are free verse or have rhyming, but there are also a few haikus and magnetic poetry thrown into the mix.

I hope you find something that speaks to you. Thank you for reading!

Amanda

Fall

Brave Souls

Dear Brave Souls,

The ones who work, smile, laugh
You carry your emotions
a badge of courage
You help others
struggle to help yourself
The world is vibrant, and crowded
A shout of laughter
is terrible
difficult to focus
on what's real and what's not
You feel suffocated
by your responsibilities

Bad Day

Having a heavy gray sort of day
The sky sucks all my energy
Icicles drip from my nose
The TV talks about frozen bodies
I can't even feel mine

The clouds weigh a million pounds
Everything shadowed in steel gray
There's this little voice deep down
It whispers, "you're worthless, you're
worthless."

Working Depressed

Drove to work in the rain
Trying to ignore the pain
Of work without sleep
Of sleep without rest
Of not feeling enough
Less than your best

The mood of the day
Is gloomy with rain
Cloudy with thoughts
Temporarily insane
Such is the life
Of the working depressed
Feeling inept
More than the rest

Warm October Whispers

Warm, October day whispers:

"Come...come and see
take a nap
underneath the trees

and if you fall into a trance
where the warm wind blows
and the leaves will dance

and you're overwhelmed
by the joy of fall
by the sun that dapples
by the birds that call

sit awhile
underneath a nice, tall tree
have a drink
and think of me."

Magnetic Poetry: Fools

peace in the world
is like when man
born naked
lived with out fire
word s or concrete
we be fools
thirsty and sad

Cages

a cubicle life
observe the humans
in their cages
one paces
tap, tap,
clickety-clack
pen slaps
chair quibbles
groan and squeal
a bark of laughter
smell of orange peel
hum of a microwave
feeding time
for the humans

Fall Is Here

Leaves are changing
Mid-September
Pumpkin spice   everywhere

Soon   mid-November
Turkey, orange
and Christmas trees

Then   late-December
God   help   us   all

Freedom

Is it so much to ask
for the freedom to create

To be my own boss
to go to work where I want
when I want
to drink coffee in my underwear

Nine to five
and suffocating
go to work and
work hard
be strong

But it doesn't feel worth it
when you feel chained to your responsibilities
I want to see that horizon

Is it so much to ask?
Is it so much to ask?
To want to be able to keep alive
my creativity?

Rules

Shadows creep, winter chills
Open closets are unkind
To the wandering mind
Of children just beginning

Mental Health Day

She shows up to work with a purple eye
"Car accident," she says and prods gingerly at
her cheek
"Someone rear-ended me, didn't notice the
stop sign."
Didn't notice me

But her friends at work notice
"She must be a terrible driver
to have so many car accidents," someone says
"Terribly unlucky," I say.
Unlucky in love, we all think.

"I was pretty shaken up," she says
and rubs her right shoulder
There's a bruise there we can't see
But no one can truly hide the bruises on their
face

"I just needed a mental health day, you know."
she smiles a weak smile, winces as she shrugs
that bruised shoulder
she looks at us
through us   searching
With eyes that see and see   and never land

Nature's Party

Then like that
it was October
days are shorter
the air is colder

The leaves blush red
and orangey-yellow

Do the trees know they'll
be naked soon?

Haiku: Fall

Riotous color
red orange pops in sunlight
leaves crumple and fall

Magnetic Poetry: Every Fortune

every fortune in this world
is secret
we live with treasure
be deep and strong
to see it

Underneath

Underneath the job title
a bunch of broken people
he's socially awkward
her husband died
she lost a baby that no one knows about
her marriage is in shambles
he's got a story to tell
anger and heartbreak, a tiny jail cell
pasts that stay hidden
desires, and oily thoughts
we hide our devastation
a work-place facade
to avoid humiliation
as we trudge along
head bowed, shattered, and bought

Solitary

Ever have the feeling that you're
the last person on earth?

(This isn't it)

alone is alone
It is hard to escape your headspace

Most people you look through
don't know you are suffering

Most people don't realize
you *wish* you were the last person on earth

But really you feel nothing
you wonder: how can nothing suffer?

Monday Blues

Monday yawned and stretched
and I with it

Maybe a quarter of a minute behind

Five days with no pay, she said
because you're not full time
you're not full pay, and you work overtime
and overtime...with no benefits

Then it hits me all at once
someone is dying
and you are sitting at work
typing out someone else's
life disappointments

You should be living
remembering and visiting
not dying yourself
at a slow, data-filled death

A few words, a comforting smile
everything's alright
but boy, they don't know how fake it is
how your 'allergies' are really tears
running down your face

and everywhere is just aching, aching, aching

with no benefits to living with a hole
you can't fill

Nature Walk

I pulled my headphones out of my ears,
I hear peepers, birds chirping, and a squirrel
scurrying up a tree

But what's the point of nature,
if the sounds of traffic drown out the joys of
life

Here's a tree, there's a tree
they might as well be plastic trees
and rubber plants
and there's the way of life
of technology
of treasures
of things that are real but are long forgotten

When I walk in the woods,
it reminds me of my childhood
the crickets are the sounds I fell asleep to
the birds chirping a mid-afternoon melody
sounds of the trees clapping back and forth
and me on my quilt in the sunshine,
falling asleep to the music of silence
of trees chattering and chattering
and always getting the last word

Walking in Cemeteries

I like walking through cemeteries
The dead are quiet
peace and birds and secrets
whispered between leaves

Sometimes sadness
hollows through the weathered tombstones
But when the sun is out
and the leaves are chattering

I feel respect
All the respect

Magnetic Poetry: Break Up

the women laugh
you smile
I listen and remember
it s not brilliant to lie
with perfume
and coffee

We Who Are Human, I Wonder

We who are human
who walk with eyes
we tell jokes
and crippling lies

What makes us 'us'?
why do we stand?
why do we sing?
or walk on land?

To be human
to know how to cry
to travel the earth
and live under sky

I wonder if somewhere
the trees are blue
someone else responds
to the names of me or you

They look at the sky
and wonder out loud
if beyond the sky
above the clouds

There lives someone else
in the great unknown
so different from theirs
another place called home

October Twenty-Fifth

Gloomy, dark Friday
Week before Halloween
Decorations come out
Orange, black and green

The witches are flying
And skeletons dance
You find that wig that matches perfectly
With those bell bottom pants

Pumpkins get new faces
Their guts thrown in the trash
Somehow, every costume you see
Is showing more...sass

There's Pumpkin EVERYTHING
We even eat the seeds
Pumpkins are the turkeys of October
But it's candy that I need!

Twix and Butterfingers
Three Musketeers, Milky Way
This diabetic would dive into a vat of chocolate
(Big sigh) ...Maybe someday

But I digress
Week before Halloween
Sky gray and spooky
Trees shed their leaves

Then, tongue on hand
And cold, doggy nose
Happiness is a tail wag
A soft warm face, pressing close

You can give me October
The bare bones left of July
But I'll keep my summer
Tucked away, just in case, (another big sigh).

Writer's Block

laundry rumbling
coins tossed
old woman gives a dirty look
you got too close to her load of whites
be wary of the red sock
and the older man who smells like peppermint
he's hogged all the washers next to you
the room is practically empty

grumpy woman eyes the bras and nighties
the delicates that can't be assaulted in the
dryer
the hum and the drone and the constant
bumping
of machines grinding back and forth

and I try to write
to disappear in a world full of magic and
demons
and fail...miserably

Bad Start

It's difficult not to sleep all day
when the dreams are more lively
than the real world outside

How does one break out of the habit
of one's own reality?
Can you make an exception?
For one's accidental inception?
Or maybe that's what I need

Come Leo, show me where the real world lies.

Apocalypse

I don't write as often as I should
Lies are told and morning comes
Some days, it's not just 'all right'

Get your coffee and corruption
Truth bleeds through your TV set
Big Brother knows and shows
What it can, when it can
And we believe

Soon, it'll be WWIII
and gas and war without the Nazis
Soon we'll die and succumb
Always under everyone's thumb

Dark days are coming you know
Can't you just feel the cold?
Big Brother tells us what to feel
And it'll snow, and snow, and snow...

Halloween

A devilish grin
bats shriek
shutters clatter
an old door creaks

Pumpkins and spiders
crawl up your back
heart starts racing
branches clatter and snap

Skeletons are dancing
bones shivering cold
witches and goblins
and buildings so old

Blood-dripping vampires
mummies and ghosts
monsters and zombies
(they scare me the most)

Kids trick-or-treating
things slimy and green
having fun being scared
now that's Halloween!

Something Else

A moment
full of something
can't describe it

Here, words aren't enough
and all you can think of
is sunlight,
aquamarine skies
and water that laps
against ankles

This is the dream world
the fantasy of a life
somewhat different

This is the feeling
of flying away
launching yourself
into someone's arms

This is the feeling
of knowing that
you're someone special

Of knowing
that you want someone else
to know it, too

Hair down, and sun on face

big grin, and big smile
so full of happiness
it takes a poem
to recognize it

Ah, there's the dream
of living someone else's life
to the fullest

Magnetic Poetry: Survival

smile and

eat life

and never wake

Isn't Enough

When something feels like nothing
doubts, hopeless feelings
that maybe you aren't good enough
exhaustion, like maybe
you're just not right for this

It's hard to tell anyone, though
they only see what's on the outside
it's hard to believe a friendly face
could be suffering

She wears a brown, fuzzy sweater
her eyes are blue and full of life
but maybe underneath
you see her fingernails are really paint-chipped
the lips wobble
smudge on her dark pants
eyeliner is beginning to run

Her mind runs a marathon everyday
her heart is squeezed in two
maybe breathing isn't as second nature
as it should be

You might feel like you know her
you might feel like
nothing can be as complicated
as what you see on the outside

but you don't hear
what her whole self is saying
behind the smile

When Tuesdays Feel Like Mondays

How I wish for a glorious sunrise
How I wish I could sleep late
But work it drones on and on
Only thirty minutes past eight

A steel gray sky and donuts
Coffee as black as can be
Yesterday's sweater and messy bun
Yes, this is definitely me

Click of the mouse and fluorescents
Fake laughs and people so happy
Sometimes you just want to slap 'em
Especially on a day so crappy

The Sunday Night Blues

Feeling the Sunday night blues
don't you
Feeling that aching, shaking feeling
of a Monday come new

It crawls into your coffee cup
It labors and delays
It's the groan you have when you wake up
It gets into your way

And if you try to hurry
The blues will get you down
You cannot run, you can't escape
A constant dragging frown

It's the Sunday night blues that'll eat you up
that continue on Monday
It'll crawl into your coffee cup
and delay, delay, delay

Winter

Snow on Trees

like a giant
dusted with a powdered wig
you rise majestically
above the ground
which crumbles under the
weight of your power

My Evil Twin Doubt

Meet my evil twin
I call her, Doubt
she second guesses
Things I've figured out

She makes me weak
When I take a stand
Kicks me down
And takes command

Invites her friends:
Anxiety and Depression
Inside I'm roiling:
I've made a bad impression

Anxiety whispers to Doubt and
Depression behind my back
They're making fun of me!
There's nothing that I lack

I am Beautiful and Strong
Creative and Inspired
My evil twin, Doubt
Is not even desired

She's shallow and she's needy
Her friends are much worse

Dripping black negativity
Tucking extra in her purse

She'll swagger up the street
People spring out of the way
Heels clicking, eyes like daggers
With nothing great to say

SAD (Seasonal Affective Disorder)

Age twenty-eight
Feels like eighty-two
Tired and achy
Like I've got the flu
One step forward
Two steps back
With joints that ache
And bones that crack
With blurry eyes
And pounding head
"I want to sleep!"
"Sleep when you're dead!"

Find Your Joy

Find your joy
on the darkest days
when the days are short
and the nights are long
when it feels like
all you can do
is wrong
Find your joy

I look to family
soft, puppy nose
colors of winter
I find my joy

In-warmth-like-love
all wrapped up
happiness is
my babe, the pup

Laughter in the kitchen
favorite TV shows
days off work
when it snows

I find my joy
shopping online
sipping tea in the bookstore
on days I feel fine

In walks after work
with the dog and his toys
long chats on the phone
these littlest of joys

Are bright tokens
of happiness
all stored away

I find my joy
on these darkest of days

Loser

five letters
of worthlessness

Lonely
Outcast
Socially Inept
Every misstep
Relapse

not a state of being
it is felt

Magnetic Poetry: Young Writer

a young woman
born with desire
she listen s
each word
is a secret
a window to
open sky s
and a vast world

Ode To Snow

Snow, you dreadful thing,
why do you fall the way you do?

Tell me, Snow, you white, white Snow,
as pale, pale white as the moon,

Would you rather melt in springtime,
then get crushed on the roadside, too?

You foolish Snow, so stupidly white,
that glitters in the sun,

Why do you have to come out and ruin
all the springtime and winter fun?

Why fall from gray-white clouds
only to sting and melt on my nose?

While the dignified rain just drips,
and does not look like dandruff on my clothes.

Snow, you bitter chill,
I'm afraid I've had enough,

of damp, damp wetness, icy chills,
and all that cold-wet stuff.

So, Snow, if you would be so kind,
please gather where I can see...

And if by mistake, I take out a few flakes...
well then, whoops, don't blame me.

The Almosts

Some are afraid of the boogie man
of the things that go bump in the night
of black sludge creeping down walls
of dark eyes, green or yellow
but what scares me the most
what haunts me
are the ghosts
the almosts, the maybes
the never-afters
the chances missed
because you swerved
when you were meant to drive straight
these uncertainties
ridicule and torture
again
and again
and again

To Dream

to sleep, perchance to dream
ah, there's the problem

to dive into another reality
one we choose not to wake from

sometimes the dreams are more than dreams
sometimes they are nightmares
sometimes they are all we have
in moments of sorrow

but if we dream forever
if we cling to the almost
the maybes, the ever-afters
we might not wake up

Bored At Work

time oozes by, with anxiety-ridden finality
the ticking of the clock was never this precise
seasons come and seasons go   some day

I'll wipe the dust from these shoulders

Animal Eyes

her eyes look hungry, frightened
he's privately amused everyday
she scurries through the door
he moves slow, like a turtle
there's a deep voice, face like a rock
a mountain of a man
shows no emotion
he treads soft, feet like a fox
she wears her pregnancy
like a fierce tigress
she starts like prey, in the copy room
we wear our faces
like animals do
never hiding
our true nature

Snowy Mornings

I like snowy mornings
not so much the drive in
slush, dirty snow, and ice
scraped off windshields

But more so that
the world is still trying to
catch its breath
after the sky has seeped
all over the landscape

Cars creep
Phones are quiet
The wind still spitting

Everyone is late
Even the snow doesn't know
it's overstayed its welcome

Finally
A day where everyone is behind
like me
and I'm not behind everyone else

8am

8am on Saturday
no one around
in a college town

windows covered in frost
car starts with a grumble
eyes bleary and lost

Coffee boils and steams
the only life stirring
are the birds

Borrowed Time

Tomorrow

Tomorrow

Tomorrow

Three alarms
In three successions

Yesterday was bliss
Today was boring

Tomorrow is always
In
The
Morning

A Christmas Plant

Red and green leaves
on a plant that's
leafy tall
stand rooted in rich brown soil
its base wrapped in green tin foil
with leaves tipping outward and stretching
like an open baseball glove

Catch the light

Catch the light

Magnetic Poetry: Cracked

like you say
each soul
is a beautiful sentence
some paragraph s give hero es
or inspire a villian
this world
like the plot
to an epic fiction
has crack ed

Twenty-Eight

Twenty-eight and dreading thirty
life is one long road...often dirty
find a job, get married, buy a house
soon you're a stay-at-home-mouse
your hair is gray, your children grown
husband retires, then you're both at home
you're growing old and grandkids, too
then you'll remember you had things to do
you wanted to travel, to see the world
paint a masterpiece, get your hair curled
dance in a rainstorm and write a play
walk across Paris on a sunny day
But time passes with each dollar spent
hair turns white; back and shoulders bent
soon you're back wishing you were twenty-
eight
but it's a wish that came just a little too late.

Silence

The cancer was naked on her skin
She looked at the stars
"Would you love me if I was bald?"

When Old Times Become New

Family visiting
Played pinochle
Feels normal
Like old times

But there's a voice
Missing from the room

And it's a large voice

Laughter and a flash
of eyes full of mischief
Light glinting off a
pair of large glasses

Do I remember the sound
of the voice those glasses
belong too?

Or is that why I'm sad?

The heart rebels when
life moves on and family grows up

We've only got each other now

But man, that house seems quiet
with one less voice
filling up the room

Too Young

Just when you think it's alright
Plans get canceled and
everything goes pear-shaped

Yesterday you felt on top of the world
Today you want to crawl under it

Yesterday you felt confident,
beautiful
Today you felt like someone else's
leftovers

And the harder you try
to climb on top of it all
You sink lower and lower and lower
an emotional oblivion

All week long you felt
that you would die young

You smelled the air,
You breathed in sunshine, loved
and felt grateful

All week long you had a feeling
in the pit of your stomach

Call it leftover anxiety
from months of procedures
and no answers

It gnaws and gnaws
at the guts of your insides

And maybe you'll die young tomorrow

Or in another 50 years

Either way
it's never enough

Time to breathe and time to die

Either way
We all die a little too young

Summer in January

It's summer in January
And not yet spring
Bugs are buzzing
Birds starting to sing

It's summer in January
January the 12th
Winter coats hung up
Gloves on the shelf

Shovels lean useless
Tucked in a corner
Days boil like liquid
Warmer and warmer

"It feels strange," says Michael
He stands at the window
"It's climate change-"
He gives me a look. "I know."

"This shouldn't be happening..."
"I know, but it is."
"Think of Australia
warmer than this."

The animals burning
Woods filled with fear
It's only January
The start of the year

Death in the middle east
(We'll see how that goes)
As snow turns to mud
and poverty grows

It's summer in January
Let's go for a walk
Pretend we're not restless
While we have a long talk

We'll say we're thankful
It's not bitterly cold
But it's summer in January
Where is the snow?

Magnetic Poetry: A Pie in the Sky

may I ask you this
do you see life
as a pie in the sky
or is it like old coffee
hard and wet

more broken than liquid
lingering but not hot
for me it's not about eternity
but almost like me
picturing cake
and eating it too

Work

There are dead souls
In the break room
I can practically hear
The shrieking
Cue the suspenseful
Horror music
And the blood
Dripping down
The walls

That there's boredom
And people's lives
Ebbing away
Can't you just
Hear the monotony?

This one's dead
And that one dying
And who
Gives a crap anyway?

Hear them whisper:

No one
No one
No one

On Vacation

I like texture
on a desktop photo
the promise
vacation leaves

florescent-bright
like sunlight
fan chopping
an ocean breeze

office chairs
become lawn chairs
coffee cocktail
clutched in hand

on the beach
out of reach
I relax my toes
in carpet-sand

Under the Influence

I fell in love
a thousand times
the night your lips
touched my neck

with sticky, pink lip gloss
tight, blue leggings
you thought I looked
like some kind of
sexy, college angel
I said you were drunk
you laughed

Then you held my hand
Under a sky that
looked like blue eye shadow

your voice was smoky

I knew
what had kissed me

Heartbreak Feels

heartbreak
time given
love lost
to move on
without you

heartbreak
the color yellow
sometimes ugly
possible bright days ahead

heartbreak
feet like lead
days stuck in shadow
heart beats a
heavy, tuneless, solo

when it hurts to breathe
when the smell of shampoo
has you sobbing in the grocery store

we store our memories
with time and love
and heartbreak

Guilt

enter a bookstore
isn't this just a sanctuary
of written thoughts
and quiet nooks
with no judgement
or weird looks

fingers trail over paperbacks
science-fiction you've never read
till you find a treasure
convince yourself
you need it desperately
it's all in your head

you're going to read it
as soon as you get home
you'll cherish it forever

but on the floor
in a plastic bag
it sits alone

Distraction

Just when you think
you are important
words tumble forth
he wants to know
wants to hear
just me and only me
a devil's grin
chugs some more beer
and then

You feel the fool
because you thought
you were special

Or is he the fool
because he sees
just the ordinary

Magnetic Poetry: New Year's Resolution

secret desire s

vast sky s

young thirsty kiss es

explore life joy

and the world

Can't They See I'm Drowning

I don't feel good enough
for the rain to touch my skin

I'm not worthy of the catharsis
of nature's natural tears

I wonder what I look like on the outside
when the minutes crawl by like years

Unrest that spins like sickness
behind my eyes
I smile, I laugh, I tease
Why can't they see the lies?

A blackness that crushes
a gray that claws
picks at your attention
pulls at your senses
clouds around your personal bubble
'til everything and everyone is in a fog

But I've got to smile
be courteous, communicative
and cooperative

I've got to be
energetic and organized

to be impossibly awesome
like no one has before

watch me drag my feet across the floor

Can't they see I'm drowning?

Cold and Tired

Heavy-lidded
Needing sleep
Dreaming of food
Counting sheep
Almost noon
No ringing phones
Tired and dead
Want to go home
Drink some water
Play with hair
Get up and walk
I can't go anywhere
Want to snuggle
A warm body will do
Once I'm in bed
I'll be down 'til two!

At the Bus Stop

If the green letters had said: "HELL"
I would have got on with a smile.

Everything was black
the pavement   the sky
the interior of the bus as it came
barreling through that hyperspace
neon green letters,
flashing its destination

I tipped my head back
and the snowflakes falling
were like
that song that I used to sing as a child
to catch snowflakes on my tongue

To jump up and down, tongue out, spinning
and spinning
To shout at the top of my lungs

But I wasn't alone with my thoughts anymore
Other students came trudging
up through the wet on the sidewalk
wet faces and wet noses and wet boots
and gloved hands and wool caps,

The darkness on their faces
pierced suddenly by the yellow flashing light
of the truck with the giant snowplow

And it made me think of an ambulance
with its dreading reds and whites

And just as I thought this
the campus clock struck nine
and made me think
how quickly happiness comes
before it is chased away

Difficult

I used to write poetry
It would come out okay
My days were not lonely
I always knew what to say

Now it's a struggle
Hard to say what I feel
Everything is a question
and feels too real

I used to be witty
To find joy in the bad
Now the clouds grow darker
and the world is so sad

It's hard to find the sweet
in the gray and the gloom
Hard to pull out the words
when there isn't the room

It's hard to find the joy
when you can't even breathe
And it's hard to create
when you do not feel free

Cold As Hell

It sucks away
the space
from your body
dry, frigid fingers
of darkness
pierce and scrape
your skin
carve canyons
of misery that bleed
and crack

March's Last Hurrah

crunchy, crunchy
snowbank
liquid white
and falling

boots and mittens
sniffly noses
cheeks beet-red
with shoveling

kids and sleds
where's the car?
winter's last hurrah
...in March.

Spring

Something New

A dry leaf skates by
pulled by the wind
which is melting

Edged with cold, and fresh
wants to be warm
but isn't quite there yet

I should walk
but I'm lulled into
this peaceful contemplation

The sun warm, the air cool
I could just nap and sleep
and finally let go

When the snow melts
When the ice pulls back
There's so much room left in the world

Dandelion

the life of a dandelion
lasts a few days
one day to burst open
as yellow sun rays

they claim a whole yard
the puffiest of weeds
until time tells them
to dissolve into seeds

Drip, Drip, Drop

Drip, drip, drop, goes the water in the sink.
As I stand there listening, it gets me to think:
How much water is in the ocean,
when the waves all dip in motion,
is it as great as I imagine,
or a waste?
Does the sunlight on the water glisten?
Can you smell its salty taste?

Drip, drip, drop, goes the water when it rains.
Flowing down rusty gutters and down shiny
windowpanes.
It gathers in wide, muddy puddles.
It clears away the dust.
It drips on plants and worn-out metal,
And gathers where it must.

Drip, drip, drop, goes the water in the sink.
As it is wasting, it gets me to think.
How much water will be needed,
When our whole supply is depleted?
When our water just flows out the drain?
There will be no waves in motion,
because there is no ocean, or water...to form
rain.

Morning, Love

Nothing more sexy
than an early morning
roll over, sleepy smile
"Morning, babe"
One semi -foggy look
bare chested and rough hair
beard thick and hand-touchable
God, I love the deep brown
eyes that crinkle and beckon
smooth skin and warmth
so luxurious and sink into
until there's nothing more natural
than saying, "Good morning"
to the one you love

Rare Books

I collect rare books
like a rich woman collects diamonds
worn and dusty covers
are jewels of knowledge
and gems of the future

Ants

ants in the tiles
beneath your toes
they crawl between your smile
and shuffle in your nose
next, they're doing the hula
on your bathroom sponge,
they're shimmying, they're shaking
having loads of fun!

Springtime Peepers

Just past the tree line
is frog church

Where Springtime water
dresses up slick bodies

Eyes shine with moonlight
Throats belt and sing
Hallelujah

At frog church
they worship the pond
they grow babies in

Twenty-nine

Twenty-nine and almost thirty
life is one long road, often dirty.
find a job to save some dough
then it's paying bills, school loans you owe
twenty-nine and splitting rent
and if you don't, money is spent
on food, electric and a car to drive
to get to work, to stay alive
those houses you imagined
with their little white fences
is another lost dream,
in the mountain of expenses
Just for a moment, you're almost there
then you break a bone, on crappy health care
the road is dirty at twenty-nine
but all the refuse, isn't mine.

Rainy Afternoon

Friday rain and pancakes
squeaky boots and gray sky
one writer's voice
a door creaks
slowly opens and deep breath
nothing there but a cup of tea,
a much-read book and rumpled covers
the stories we tell
when the day is long
and the leaves are wet
and the road is slippery
when a curtain is ruffled
and the air smells of dirt, and worms and
springtime
are the adventures we dream of
when the day slumbers on
a rainy afternoon

Magnetic Poetry: Innocence

women do magic
young men blush
breathe sad broken smile s
and listen
their liquid eye s naked
with longing

Live, Live

Periods of inspiration
filter through my day
in the shower
while driving
(usually on the highway)
no pen or paper
texts in my phone
fifteen emails a day

But then there are moments
where inspiration
is like the stale
breath on your lips
something about it
reeks of everydayness
of something generalized
like every other boring sap
who stinks of garbage mouth
you brush and you scrub
and you try to feel like new again
with the shiny pieces
sparkling through with imagination
like childhood

Very few I think
forget as an adult
that childhood imagination
shouldn't be shunned
but cherished
like a feeling of new-age revival

Bring out the broken pieces
repair them with relish
remember that you don't
work to die
you make money
to live, and live and live
to be carefree
and use time wisely

Haiku: Margarita Thursday

olives, salt, sugar
the perfect margarita
washing away stress

Blue

I'd like to write about an ocean day
where you can stick your toes in the sand
the waves make music; the birds will cry
where you shed away the day's demands

Each ocean wave is a symphony
an orchestra of blues and greens
sand between toes, an artist's dream
a blanket of softness, surrounds

Observe the birds, the bright blue sky
the curve where the land meets the water
watch the day's demons go floating by
"You forgot your swimsuit? Ohh, it doesn't
matter!"

Your beach is private, your view is too
and your thoughts can go on forever and ever
There's no limit to what you can do
you can tackle any endeavor!

To own my own beach, is a glorious thought
to find myself there, is better
one is a dream, possibly bought
Reality is quite a bit wetter

Open

I miss Spring
and new beginnings
I was a baby born
at the right time
my time comes
when the weather is warm
and the sky is breathing
and the trees and flowers
open up and bloom

They stretch
and I stretch
try to hug the sky
and envelope myself in
the atmosphere of nature

If I could fade away
and be a piece of earth
I would be a flower
or a star in the sky
either way, someone looks up
or you open and shine

Big Picture

In a painting I bought grandma
there stands a white-gray crane
in the middle of an orangey-brown swamp

Above the tree line,
white clouds arc across a blue sky
first, large and white, then fluffy
then small in the distance
no more than a memory

I am that broken record
remembering memories in an old picture
Remembering
Wondering
how often she stood
in the middle of everything
solitary and sturdy
the mother of all cranes

Now all that's left
is a painting I'd given her
Does she stand alone still?
Does her strong, regal head turn
to look down that skyline?

Maybe so

Or she *is* the skyline
the water, the leaves, the trees

In death,
a lonely bird can transcend time
In life,
she sits and waits

What does it mean to fly?

Her audience mourns her regal procession
not realizing that life
really is just one big intermission
the real show happens after

But I am a fool
sadness breaks
and I yearn for an encore
without the crane in the painting
the picture collapses

Of Forgetting

like bits of fluff
important stuff
comes and goes
as the wind blows

out one window
and then the next
to leave more room
to forget!

Not Goodbye

I remember my grandma's poppies
bright orange-red flowers
bright green stems, their petals iridescent,
like glitter on your fingertips
like you've been touched by
butterfly wings

Every year they would bloom
and every year they would die
mowed over until just the bristles remain
"They'll come back next spring,"
my mother told me,
But to me it felt like a bad joke.

I think about love
how it doesn't really go away
after you've lost someone special

Instead, it grows,
becomes that sadness
that labors in your chest

You cling to symbols:
old pictures, a key chain
a necklace she probably never wore
You tell yourself: "these things really
mattered"

But, what you should be harboring

are the memories
the tokens of life's joys and heartbreak

Dear Grandma,

Your house still smells like you
it misses the joyful, "hellos," that echo
and hugs that used to
smoosh my glasses up into my nose

I look out your bathroom window
I can still see your clothes
on the line, blowing in the wind

I can see all the picnics, all the weddings, all
the graduations, all the Christmases
will anyone every throw crumpled
wrapping paper at me again?

But still, I'll remember,
when the trees grow,
when the family members become
more strangers than friends
I'll remember that your house
is you, and this land
still hums with your presence

and your family is still here
and I am still here, and this feels like goodbye,
but how could it be?

How could it be?

Magnetic Poetry: Rainy Day

cloud s bring liquid morning s
like ocean s
like blue sky
like joy
and the soft breath
of steam to my lip s

Saying Goodbye to April

the leaves beckon "come hither"
get off your lazy bum
my trees are full
flowers tilted in bloom
tomorrow is another tomorrow
the sun shines lazily down on empty chairs
all I can hear is the rain to come
feel the cold on the back of my neck
hear the pat-pat of drops on my new umbrella

the world feels empty
if there is adventure out there
I have yet to find it

Be Aggressive

It's not in me to manipulate
it's not in my nature
to be aggressive
I am shy
I am compassionate
I am that friend to listen
to lean on
you tell me your weaknesses
I don't pounce
or take advantage

But when it comes to a job
employers want
the people who go out of their way
to be the know-it-alls
the spiders and snakes in this world

they don't hire the mice,
the things to be trodden underfoot

they don't know that underneath this timidness
is a loyalty
which surpasses
everything they've ever dreamed of
a finality
a getting things done
But
I am that smoldering lake of lava, slowly
simmering
But I pack a punch in a big way.

Heartbreak

I guess I never understood the expression:
loving someone so much that it's painful
'til now
The way you smile and your eyes light up
your teeth much straighter than mine
makes me think
you don't realize the power
that a simple touch
and a simple smile has

But falling for you
is like getting slapped
a thousand times

How do I know you won't hurt me?
with my brain, my body
the dreams of the future?
It's all a matter of trust

And that's something I don't have.

Morning Time

An early sun morning
everything growing, yearning
bits of wet
clings to the porch
bins of recycling
in the silence
breaks a soft cry
a bird's call of
good morning

Magnetic Poetry: Morning Kisses

your kiss es are delicious
let morning shiver s
melt away
in each concrete embrace

Out For a Walk

angry cars at stoplights
cat stretched out on the sidewalk
a furry checkpoint
pay the toll

(one pat, a scratch behind the ear)
and be on your way

a young girl named "Marty"
a huge, long-haired dog
looks like a four-legged Chewbacca
two women wearing name tags
clutching flyers: *Avoid eye contact*

a couple who clearly don't shower
lovely garden, though,
a guy walking his dog
tugs on a ball in his dog's mouth

water brown and stagnant
so dry, my scuffing feet
drown out the sound of running water

thoughts are racing
and breath in gasps

need to go, go, go

up one more stairs,

down two, one more to go
then back home and time
for the inhaler; breathe, breathe

breathe in the life
of a home so varied

of one walk
that took only thirty minutes

Refreshed

water rushing
like the sound of the wind
in the trees

makes me want to settle
on a blanket
in the warm grass

people splash in the lake
children laugh and play
this is just what I needed

what a perfect end
to a not-so-perfect day

Rain

Big drops in tiny puddles
leaves heavy and wet
cats shaking paws all befuddled
Let's see if it's stopped yet

Rain boots and big umbrellas
yellow coats and squeaky shoes
'round a corner, "let's splash that fella!"
Sniffly noses, colds and flus

For me: it's a good book and hot tea
quiet adventures, all alone
it's not lonely, my book and me
It's...a feeling of home.

Springtime On a Sunday

Smells like freedom
Floats through the window
Like thin cotton sheets
Beckons me to explore
Run, jump, climb
Be someone else
Except the winter bum
You've become
Be brave, be free
Be springtime
And live

The Words

Love the way
a good book feels
gets inside your skin
Makes you feel
Feel, feel
Feel as you aren't real
Feel as if you are dreaming

Love like the impossible
Forbidden
Without limits
No hesitation
Love without sleep
without barriers
nothing to keep,
keep you back
from full throttle

Love the thrill
of overkill
of too much
and not enough
Feel, feel, feel
Words so powerful
Transports you into
another time
another place

You are the impossible
You are that dream

you've started to become
and you can feel
the way it burns
inside you
Love, love, love
Until you die
Until you cry
Reach for the impossible
New beginnings.

Of Books

I bought a book
at the bookstore
I bought a book
I don't need more

Hug it close
to my chest
Dream of
quiet nights
A writer's quest

What new people
live in its pages
A girl, a boy
An army of mages

The dream's the journey
In dusty pages
A book
A store
And dreams galore

Magnetic Poetry: Every Heart

in every heart
there is the desire
to live
to love
and question
these difficult truth s

When Springtime Comes

We emerge from hibernation
Pale creatures shedding our winter coats
We sniff the warm air cautiously
Is that a bee that just floated by my head?

Springtime fuzzes are mysterious buggies
and many a headache and plugged noses
We realize how ugly the trees look
without their coverings
All gray and scraggly and worn out

At last, we think, some green and flowers
blue skies and picnics in the sun
We hope for a long spring and summer

We hope for thunderstorms and iced tea
and listening to the skies when it rains
Mostly we hope for how it was
before winter came to us

Already Walking

My mother asks me: Why don't you go for a
walk? The sun is nice and bright today

But what she does not know is that I am
already walking
at least that's what I say

I'm walking through a meadow of flowers,
there are rose scented petals on my fingertips

I lift up my face to the blue-tinted sky   and
she doesn't know
the sun's a smile on my lips

The sun warms my shoulders, the skin on my
neck
like the warmth of a blanket, heavily draped

And I smell the warm air, warm and fresh to
my nose,
as the wind rustles my hair in my face

The color around me, the beautiful roses, the
red and the green and the blue

And here I am lying, my face turned away,
while she says: why don't you?

I touched the green clover, I smelled its green
scent, the wind rustling, a purse to my lips

I'm walking through a meadow of flowers   and
she doesn't know

I'm touching the sky with my fingertips

Blue Bird Welcomes the Spring

Blue bird sits under an old, oak tree,
his head tipped back towards the sky.
He puffs out his orange-red breast,
just one last song before he flies.

Cardinals join his herald of spring;
the blue jays, too and chickadees.
Chattering squirrels chase and climb;
a cat blinks lazily beneath the trees.

Old snow melts, and drops and drips,
the trees try to shake off winter's chill.
Blue bird watches, and waits, and sits;
the air is fresh, the earth is still.

The winter was cold, harsh, and long;
a woman shovels a snowy drive.
She welcomes the cheerful bird-song,
she loves the sound of feeling alive.

Feet away, under an old oak tree,
blue bird sits, and watches, and waits.
Sunlight touches his breast and beak,
he shakes his wings of one last snowflake.

Summer

Something Missing

A boy kicks a hacky sack
outside Alphabet Soup, toy shop
on that liberal side of town

You can be surrounded by people
and feel so lonely
Smell of incense, wet dirt
live music, sounds nice
the summer night, to tell a story
a story filled with heartbreak, regrets and new
memories

Security is an old man with an empty coffee
cup
Families are diverse, and couples walk
unashamed with tattoos and purple hair
The singer croons and someone in the crowd
whistles
And I think that this night feels
perfect, almost

The seat next to me is empty
And just as a write this – someone whistles
But it's not you, babe. It's not you.

Deep Thoughts

Looking for inspiration
I turn to God
"Why did you build the stars?"
Mike hears and says, "Years, babe.
Years and years."
I turn to science then,
"Let's go to Mars!"
Mike hears
"It's too far,"
he says. "Too far."

I think about how round the sun is
How it burns with that blazing yellow
How there are patterns in a turtle's shell
That weren't there when it was born

How there is space junk swirling around earth
Like that ball and string on a pole
Waiting to smack you in the face

"Why is the earth round?"
Mike looks at the ground
At me, all around, and gestures
"To contain all of this."

And I snuggle in close and smile.

Heavy

Blinking awake
with a start, you realize
the weight of the ceiling
is closer than you thought

Hot

Today's sky is sweating
heavy clouds
are furrowed brows

The air that sticks
molasses thick
sucks and clings
to everything

Insomnia

Cannot sleep
all the words of today
keep rattling around
like
yesterday's old news

Life's unfair
you quickly learn
and anyone who cares
are the wrong sort of people

I want to dream
of someplace warm
plant my toes in sand
feel the smooth sift
of memories
curled around my toes

Life's a mystery, ain't it?

A drawn-out affair

It's not worth it
to lose sleep
over something so petty

To live in a fair world
ah, there's the dream

Up and Up

Grandma always wanted to ride
on a hot air balloon

This summer at a festival
I bought a key chain

Colors of the rainbow
colors so obnoxious
so bright and clown-like

But every time I drive
or look down at my keys
unlocking the apartment door
I am reminded of a dream

Grandma was too sick
she couldn't go
balloons go too high
and the air was too cold
but not this time

Balloons go up and up
they are bucket list dreams
and that's my goal
the desire
to not let life pass me by

Always be on that balloon
that's going somewhere

Empathy

So you meet empathy and
Ain't she a witch
with her awkward goodbyes

Inside your feeling
sick; stomach recoils
What can I say?
What can I say?

A pleasure to meet you
But why the hell do you care?

Get rid of your thoughts of kill,
your mindful suicide

The Writer

To make love to a writer
is like being in the presence
of a rare and beautiful creature

Her eye is like that of a bird's
Her wingspan, glorious, iridescent
She is the light that shivers
across the sheen of colors,
She is something fabulous, new
and exotic

She'll take flight and soar
across the empty spaces
alight on a branch, both close
and so far away at the same time.

She is watching and waiting
for the new opportunities
forever the observer
forever alone

Magnetic Poetry: Writing Poetry

sacred word s
cloud s like candy
green coffee
and ice breeze s
we explore more than some
every naked thought
open to each of us
and we listen
to life s joy
and sad time s

The Stars

I have known them all
Have seen them fall
Inky black
And glittering

Round, ablaze
An endless gaze
Parts unknown
Obliterating

Rocks that wink
From blue to pink
Catching minds
Illuminating

The Farmer

Old and tired
he trudges his way
out the door
his shoulders droop
as if from a great burden
his eyes a distant blue

Ask him about the past
and he'll say, "we all make our choices."
I wonder if he thinks:
"I regret mine."

But you would never know it

Gray is the hair
that peppers his scalp
white is the color of his beard

Brown is the color
of the wrinkles
under his eyes
the tired bags there, are purple

He lugs all these colors
with an air of sadness
I think of Eeyore
his sad tired way of speaking

I think of hard work
and many years gone

and I want to slump along with him

Brown and black are the colors
of the stains and scars
on his fingertips
twenty years of hard work
etched forever in his skin

But amongst the gloom
his laughter breaks
a sunshiny yellow
a deep belly laugh
with the occasional snort

It's good to have a sense of humor
in a tired life
because life
doesn't always turn out how you want it to

Hair Salon

what's better than hanging out
at the hair salon with a girlfriend
on a Saturday night

dreaming about summer
wishing our hair was long and
yellow as the sunshine
on our faces

thinking of the long drives
up the hill
when summer lasted a year
full of lightning bugs
and crickets humming

when he put his arm around me
whispered against my neck
"there's only you, and no one else"
and my heart pounded
my breath caught

and I felt young, and so alive

so alive

Nap Time

The wind blows soft through my window
I can feel the heat of the day outside
so seductive, so smooth
like the down of a baby duckling
like a kitty-cat
like my bed that I'm lying on right now
so familiar, so right
I sniff at my blue-green comforter,
and it smells like sunshine
like nap time
Oh yes, like nap time

Magnetic Poetry: Saturday Night

we dazzle
and explore
buried our god s
and every dance
and after smile
was like blue liquid
and wild fire in our belly s

Haiku: Train

Late at night leaving
train whistles passed my window
out of mind and time

Friendship

not money,
or life's glamour
but pure,
and helpful

A pat on the back
a warm smile
and suddenly you're not
alone anymore

I've said it before
and I'll say it again
friends really are
the family you choose

Nothing

A night of doing nothing
a nothing sort of night
eating food and TV
Let's turn out all the lights

Underneath the covers
the fan blasting on high
you turn and give a smile
your head resting on my thigh

"What do you want to do, babe?"
"Nothing," I reply
Eyes drinking in my face
I sigh and sigh and sigh

Scribbles

A writer without a notebook,
is like a painter without paint
A poet without ink
A politician who can't think
A mathematician who can't solve
A dog who can't bark
A writer can't write
An artist can't...art?
So I'll take my fingers
to the keyboard at hand
I'll write on my phone
and type what I can
It's an amazing relief
to find time for scribbles
Because writing is *voice,*
(although mine seems like drivel)

Rainy Sunday Afternoon

I like rain on a Sunday afternoon
I like the way it falls, the way it sounds
the look of green, the slick streets
the pattering sound when it hits the ground
me in my pjs, cartoons in the background
like someone stroking my hair
after a long bath in suds and warm water

Today, the darkness won't bother me
today, I will conquer the dark and the sadness
with comforting thoughts of trees filled with
raindrops
heavy with water, drooped so low over the
ground

This should be their attitude of sadness
this should be proof that the universe is low
but instead, I think of it as trees bowing
to the universe in reverence
the earth is crying
and this is their moment of silence

Next To You

Arms, hips, thighs
Legs and ankles
It's more than just warmth
Heat that simmers
Smooth skin against rough

Then it's boiling
Breath gasps
And breathing in
the chaos of
Something glorious

Chaos so beautiful
It hurts to look at
Even clichés sound better
Next to you

Magnetic Poetry: Togetherness

each warm smile
was magic
we live wild
with blazing morning s
and time s with you
that breathe and steam
an eternity young
and never old

Vegetable Lovin'

Love like vegetables
Roll around in the hay
Let's get rotten together

Connection Lost

why is it when you try so hard to reach
someone
you fail
signals off
or wasn't there in the first place

here I am
or used to be
clock ticking on the wall
ready to fall
off into oblivion

everyone growing old
and growing up
they are strangers
you'll say, "hello"
they'll say, "goodbye"
and next thing you know
you're thinking about the gap
of where the conversations supposed to be

maybe that's why I stopped trying
results never worth the effort
awkward attempts
are disastrous goodbyes

maybe next you'll be wondering why
good friends are so hard to make

it's never like the movies
the rain falls like heartbreak
but usually it just gets the streets wet

then you're walking alone
and wiping away tears
that feel like lost chances

You

Ah, man of many talents
Lover of video games
Fan of George R. R. Martin
A man of many names
Some may call you, "brother"
Parents call you, "son"
But me, babe...
(sighs)
Me, babe...
(grins)
Let's go have some fun

Library

stacks of books
quiet corners
and table nooks
the chairs are patterned
the carpet's soft
daylight beckons
Here's where we start off:

pick your destination
a rocket to space
mars like universe
a romantic place
he's on a pirate ship
she's in the sky
stomp through
castles and lakes
watch dragons fly

hiking through jungles
searching for treasure
double-secret-agent-lives
an island of pleasure

here's the adventure:
giants and elves
magic spells
risking your life
one sunny afternoon
all on bookshelves

Magnetic Poetry: And This Too Shall Pass

smile young and old
this blue morning will melt away
let joy linger with desire
fire dance into our live s
like a cool drink on a hot day
breathe it in and embrace it

Baseball Memories

If I could pick a moment
this would be it
smell of beer
shiny, blue wooden seats
smell of popcorn and
Charge!
A clean hit to left field
Aw, base runner out at first
The crowd goes wild

Your hand in mine
I grin even as my heart aches
This place reminds me of Grandma
I can see her wide grin
the way she bounced in her seat
to every little song between innings

Suddenly, I want to laugh and cry
and when the sky bursts with color
I look back at your face
My arm around my niece,
Your eyes on mine
Eyes dark, as the sky riots with light
and I know now I want to cry

Embraced by the ones I love
I am that sky coming apart in flashes and
sparkles

Trying to hold back the tears
Feeling so whole I just can't take it
and then it's over
I am an echo of happiness, of sadness
But I am something else, too

Best Friends

We lie there in a tent made of fake canvas; it
smelled like dirt and plastic and camping

and somehow, I knew this would be one of the
last times we would really spend together,
the three of us bunched up together on that
old blow-up mattress

But it wasn't evident from the stars that
twinkled down on our faces,
Or the crickets that chirped and sang...
We were alive and we were beautiful and
young,
and nothing ever got its way in our paths.

I remember asking, when did you think we
would die?
How someone went silent and then, "I never
really thought about it much."

How I replied: "I think I'll go young. It's not
like I want to, but I never really saw myself
doing much. I can't picture my future."

I remember silence and the crickets humming
and I'm sure there were lightning bugs, too,
(there's always lightning bugs).
Then someone takes a breath and we're talking
about *Twilight*, and school and boys and how

remember that time you fell in the creek, and someone was clever enough to snap a picture?

Now I look back and wonder if anyone ever knows the future? And if they do, don't they know it is more like a journey, best imagined sometimes an adventure, but always survived.

One minute it's there, and the next minute gone. A feeling like a breath, an instant, a tear drop, a thought.
Gone with last night's breeze and this morning's rough chill.

Sometimes it takes a whole minute to hold onto something, but it takes only a second to realize what it is, and then it's gone.

Sunshine

You thought I was cool
and I didn't even have to try

Like a puppy
shadowing my steps

A little sunshine
bursting with curiosity

A piece of my soul
bubbling next to mine

Making me feel special
when I didn't feel like it at all

Everything I liked
you liked, too

And new ideas were
treasures of discovery

I try to puzzle it out
what it all means

To me, it feels like this
raw band of unfiltered emotion

The very breath from my body
willing to sacrifice everything

Feeling as if I love you more
than I love myself

And that's the trick
isn't it

I forgot about myself
and...you were loving me anyway

Summary

People say there is something
about the way light shines across crystal
across diamonds, too

But there is really something to be said
about thousands of lightning bugs
on a warm June night
that makes the world glitter and take a deep
breath

These are the diamonds of the midnight
summer
these gems of remembrance
these flashes of yesterday

Maybe Someday

One good day
then the next
less than the best

Summer passes
like a fall breeze
feels nice at first
then gets colder

One day you'll think back
(as in tomorrow)
You'll think
if only I had the energy

If only I had the time
the freedom
free from thoughts
this constant eternal headache
that thinks and thinks
and sabotages

Someday
I'll get what I want

Then when I get it
I won't remember it

But it's the thought that counts
...or does it?

Someday I'll be free
of this internal monologue
That hogs the show
and has a sad ending
Someday, I'll take my final bow

...but that day is not today

I wish the trickster, who ruins the show
the heckler
would die in a pit of hellish fire
The kind that burns forever but never
consumes
Then I could be free

Free to create, free to live
Maybe I'll finally sleep
and really mean it

Maybe someday I'll be able to say what
words really mean
How they're not worth it if you're not living

Maybe I'll get my hands in and
build bridges, a mote, a breadbasket   and
tangle my fingers in impossible letters,
squish my fingers through the possibilities
like play dough or clay

Maybe someday
I'll get to
mold my future like artists do

About the Author

Amanda Joy Morse is a fiction writer and poet. She likes writing quirky, imaginative stories and hopes to write a screenplay someday. Amanda has a bachelor's degree in English Literature from Binghamton University, and lives in Upstate New York with her boyfriend and a chocolate lab named Koda.

Please visit her website at www.aj-morse.com.

Acknowledgements

A big thank you to Joshua for helping me with my many questions about self-publishing, and for lending a second eye to this manuscript. I am so glad to call you "friend."

Thank you to Jackie and Chigz; chatting with you and supporting one another has been the best thing that has happened to me during these stressful years. Seriously. I love you guys. OMUTB forever.

Thank you to Michael for telling me to get things done when I am so ready to give up half the time.

And to Koda...for all those nights where I wouldn't stop staring at my computer screen to play with you. I'm sorry buddy. Life's rough, and you're awesome. Love you.

www.ingramcontent.com/pod-product-compliance
Lightning Source LLC
LaVergne TN
LVHW051238080426
835513LV00016B/1656